SCHOLASTIC

Turn-to-Learn Wheels
ALPHABET

by Virginia Dooley

NEW YORK • TORONTO • LONDON • AUCKLAND • SYDNEY
MEXICO CITY • NEW DELHI • HONG KONG • BUENOS AIRES

Teaching *Resources*

Thanks to Jason Robinson
and Deborah Schecter

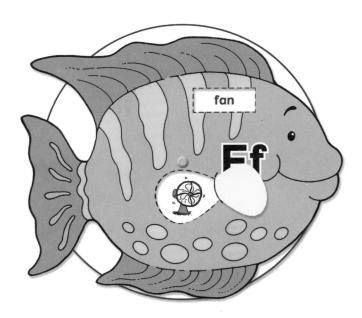

Previously published as *Turn-to-Learn Alphabet Wheels*

Cover and interior illustrations by Rusty Fletcher
Cover and interior design by Jason Robinson

ISBN-13: 978-0-545-15432-4
ISBN-10: 0-545-05432-1

1 2 3 4 5 6 7 8 9 10   16 15 14 13 12 11 10 09

Contents

Alphabet Wheels

About This Book

Welcome to *Turn-to-Learn Wheels in Color! Alphabet*. The 26 irresistible, interactive wheels in this book were developed to delight children and help you lay the foundation for reading success.

Research shows that using key picture and word associations to teach the alphabet helps children establish strong letter-sound relationships and build phonemic awareness—critical skills in becoming successful readers and writers. The adorable pictures on each wheel help children become acquainted with words that begin with each letter.

The bright colors and playful, guessing-game format invite children to use the wheels over and over, helping them get lots of practice with letter sounds and configurations. The wheels are also self-correcting, so they provide instant feedback. If a child does miss a word, a turn of the wheel provides a fresh opportunity to try again. In addition, the wheels will help children meet key language arts standards. (See page 8 for more information.)

You can use the wheels as the focus of a one-on-one lesson, place them in a learning center for children to use independently or in pairs, and even make multiple copies of each wheel for greater flexibility. (See "Using the CD," page 6, for more.) However you choose to incorporate the wheels in your classroom routine, children will enjoy this playful spin on learning the alphabet that will put them on the path to reading success!

Assembling the Alphabet Wheels

WHAT YOU NEED

- scissors
- brass fastener
- craft knife (adult use only)

WHAT TO DO

1. Each wheel consists of two parts: a window wheel and a picture wheel. Remove the pages for each wheel from the book. (If you like, glue the pages to cardstock and/or laminate them for added durability.) Then cut out both wheels along the outer solid lines.

2. Place the window wheel on a protected surface. Then use a craft knife to cut out the word window and the picture-window flap along the dashed lines. If the wheel has a sliding piece that hides the picture (for example, the elephant's trunk for the *Ee* wheel, page 25), cut that out as well.

3. Place the window wheel on top of the picture wheel. Insert a brass fastener through the crosses at the center as shown below, and open the prongs on the back to secure. If the wheel has a sliding piece that hides the picture, attach it by inserting the fastener through the white circles.

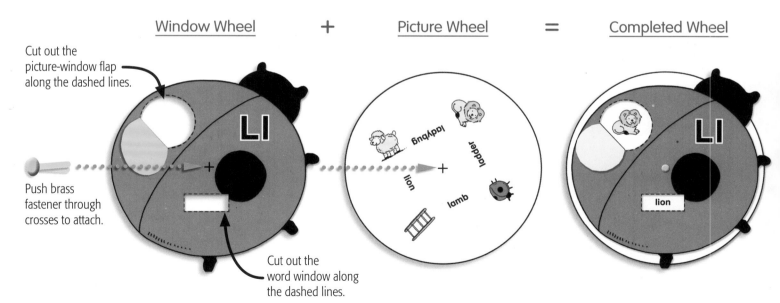

| Window Wheel | + | Picture Wheel | = | Completed Wheel |

Cut out the picture-window flap along the dashed lines.

Push brass fastener through crosses to attach.

Cut out the word window along the dashed lines.

Introducing the Alphabet Wheels

1. Show children a sample wheel, for example, the wheel for *Bb*. Invite them to identify the picture on the window wheel (a *butterfly*), and think about the sound at the beginning of this word. Then point out the *Bb* on the window wheel and read it aloud, noting the upper- and lowercase forms.

2. Show children how to turn the bottom wheel so the word *butterfly* appears in the window. Encourage them to think about the sound of the first letter and use what they know about the sounds of other letters in the word to try to read the word. They can then open the flap and see if they read the word correctly by checking the picture cue. (For wheels that have a sliding piece, children slide the piece to reveal the picture.)

3. Invite children to turn the wheel and practice reading each of the four words. Repeated practice will help children master each word and build automaticity. (Note: Each vowel wheel includes words that begin with both short- and long- vowel sounds. And because there are few picturable words that begin with the letter *X*, the words *box* and *fox* have been included on the wheel for this letter.)

4. Use the easy activites to extend learning on page 7 to help children explore letters further.

Creating Customized Wheels

● Print a copy of the window wheel for a target letter (in color or black and white) and a blank picture wheel. Cut out and assemble the wheel. Children can suggest words that begin with the target letter and draw or find pictures to illustrate the words. Children will especially enjoy seeing their own names included on the appropriate letter wheel, along with a drawing or photograph of themselves.

● Make additional wheels to focus on ending sounds. Have children suggest words that end in each sound and find or draw corresponding pictures.

Tip

The wheels work best if children turn the bottom wheel while holding the top wheel in place.

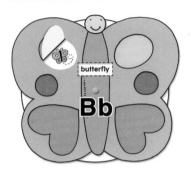

Using the CD

The CD that comes with this book includes ready-to-print versions of each of the 26 alphabet wheels in both full-color and black-line formats. It also includes blank templates for creating customized wheels. Make extra wheels to create class sets, to place in a learning center for small groups of children to explore independently, or to tuck inside backpacks to build at-home literacy.

Activities to Extend Learning

Give children additional opportunities to explore letters either before introducing the wheels or after. Here are some suggestions.

- Have children trace a letter in the air or on their arm as you say it aloud.

- Give each child a small tray of rice or sand and invite children to use their fingers to write letters in these materials.

- Children might enjoy making letters out of clay, pipe cleaners, Wikki Stix®, aluminum foil, or pieces of twigs and sticks.

- Keep an eye out for objects that are shaped liked letters. A handle on a mug might look like a *C*, for example, or a clock face might look like an *O*. Point these objects out to children and invite them to identify others that resemble letters in your classroom and at home.

- Hold a letter scavenger hunt. Challenge children to search the room for items whose names have the same initial sound as a target letter.

- Give children cups filled with alphabet pasta or cereal. Ask them to sort the letters. You might have them find as many of a particular letter as possible, or sort the letters according to various criteria, for example, vowels, consonants, letters made with all straight lines (*E, H, T, W*), letters made with all curved lines (*C, O, S, U*), or letters made with both straight and curved lines (*B, D, P, R*).

- Help familiarize children with various ways letters appear in texts compared with the way they write them. Invite them to form a letter collection by creating an alphabet letter wreath. Help them cut out the center of a large paper plate. Then have children glue on examples of a specific letter cut from magazines, newspapers, and junk mail. You might also let children use a computer to create and cut out letters in different fonts.

Meeting the Language Arts Standards

Connections to the McREL Language Arts Standards

Mid-continent Research for Education and Learning (McREL), a nationally recognized nonprofit organization, has compiled and evaluated national and state standards—and proposed what teachers should provide for their PreK–K students to grow proficient in language arts. This book's activities support the following standards:

Uses the general skills and strategies of the reading process including:

- Knows uppercase and lowercase letters of the alphabet
- Uses basic elements of phonetic analysis (e.g., understands sound-symbol relationships; beginning and ending consonants, vowel sounds) to decode unknown words

Uses grammatical and mechanical conventions in written compositions including:

- Uses conventions of print in writing (e.g., forms letters in print, uses uppercase and lowercase letters of the alphabet)

Source: Kendall, J. S. & Marzano, R. J. (2004). *Content knowledge: A compendium of standards and benchmarks for K–12 education.* Aurora, CO: Mid-continent Research for Education and Learning Online database: http://www.mcrel.org/standards-benchmarks/

Connections to Early Childhood Language Arts Standards

The activities in this book are also designed to support you in meeting the following PreK–K literacy goals and recommendations established in a joint position statement by the International Reading Association (IRA) and the National Association for the Education of Young Children (NAEYC):

- Understands that print carries a message
- Engages in reading and writing attempts
- Recognizes letters and letter-sound matches
- Begins to write

Source: *Learning to Read and Write: Developmentally Appropriate Practices for Young Children*, a joint position statement of the International Reading Association (IRA) and the National Association for the Education of Young Children (NAEYC). http://www.naeyc.org/about/positions/pdf/PSREAD98.PDF © 1998 by the National Association for the Education of Young Children

Aa

+

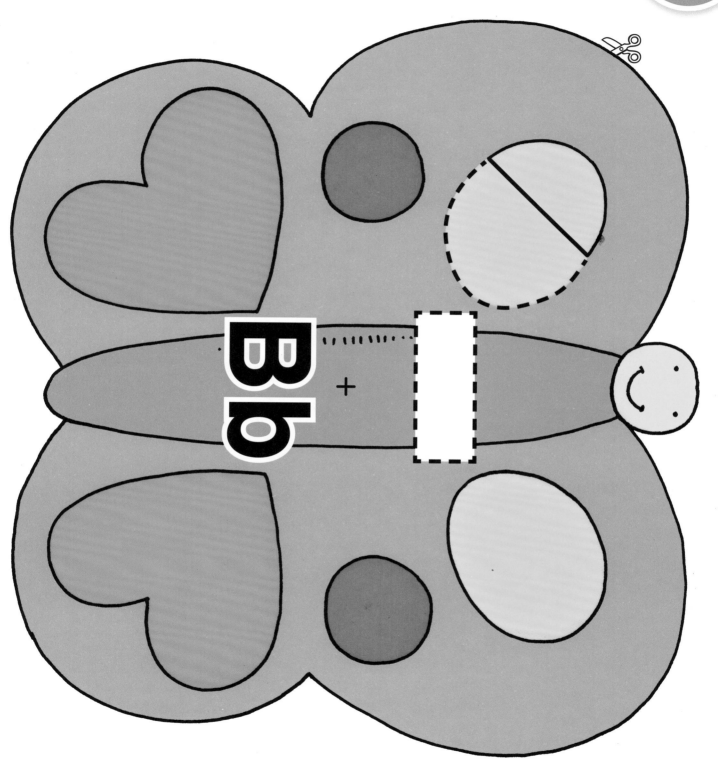

bear

butterfly

\+

boat

book

Assembled Wheel

Turn-to-Learn Wheels in Color! Alphabet © 2009 by Virginia Dooley. Scholastic Teaching Resources

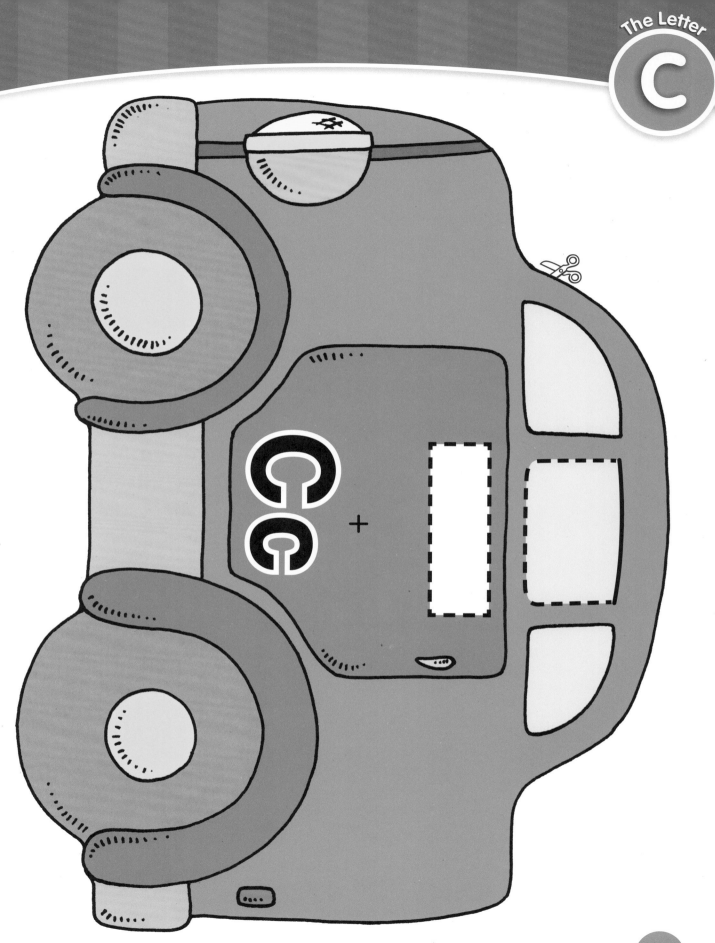

cookie

computer

+

cat

car

Assembled Wheel

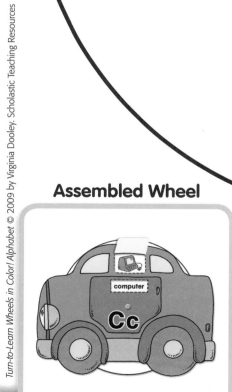

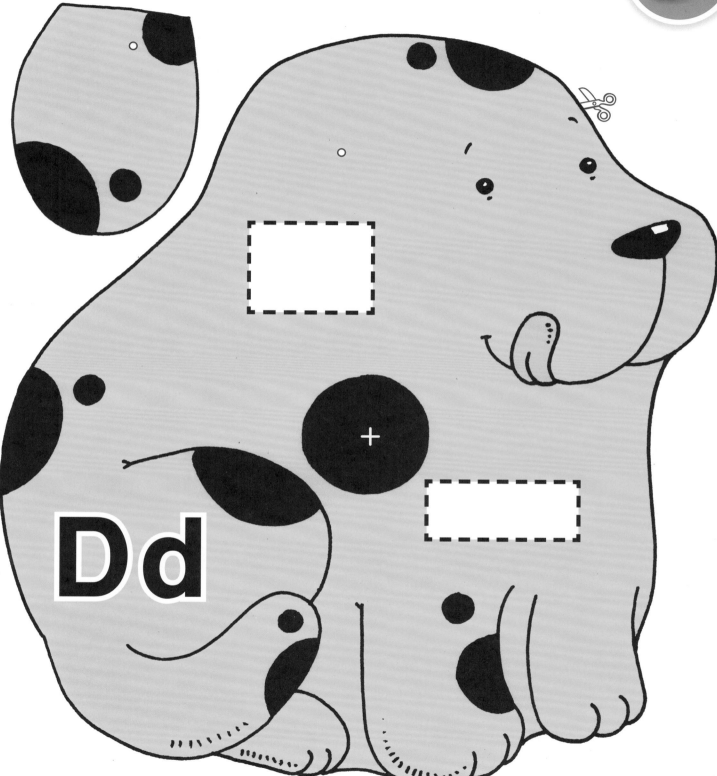

Dd

dish

doctor

+

dog

duck

Assembled Wheel

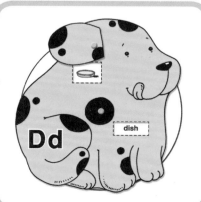

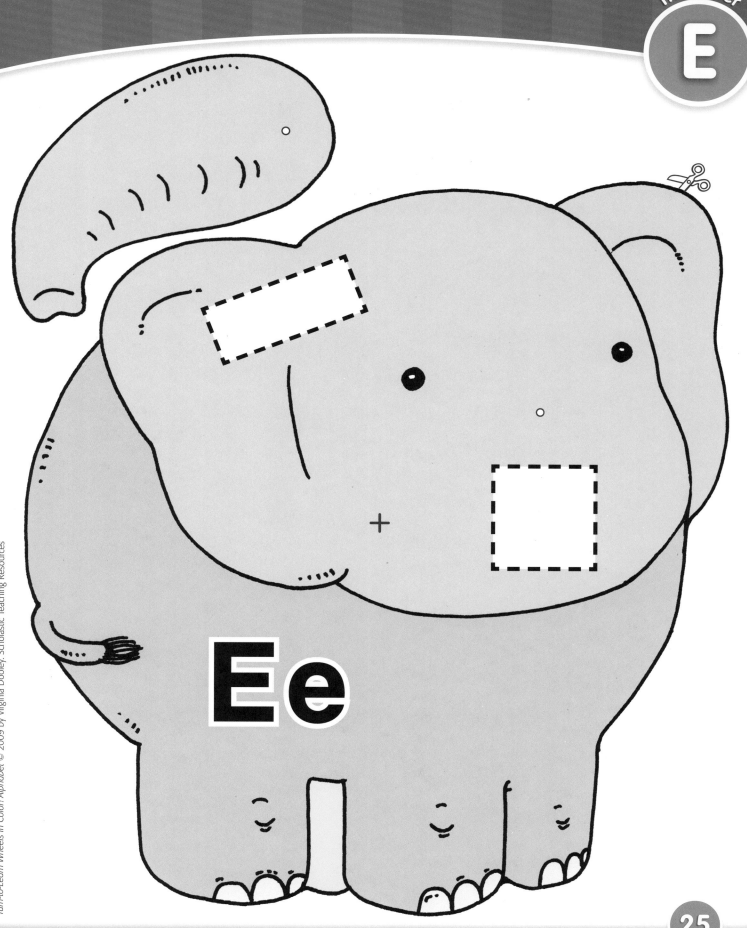

Ee

easel

elephant

egg

ear

Assembled Wheel

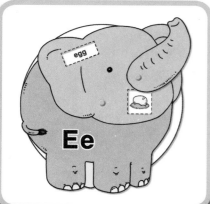

egg

Ee

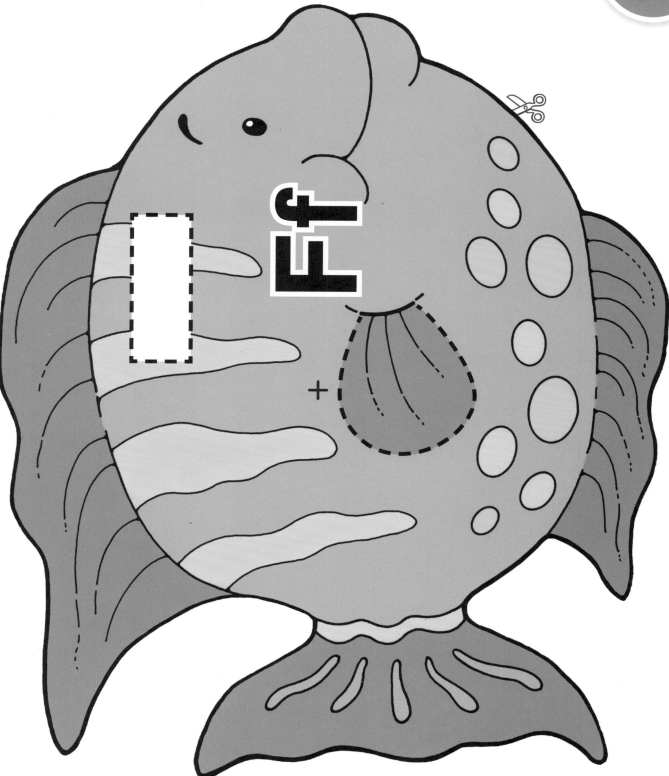

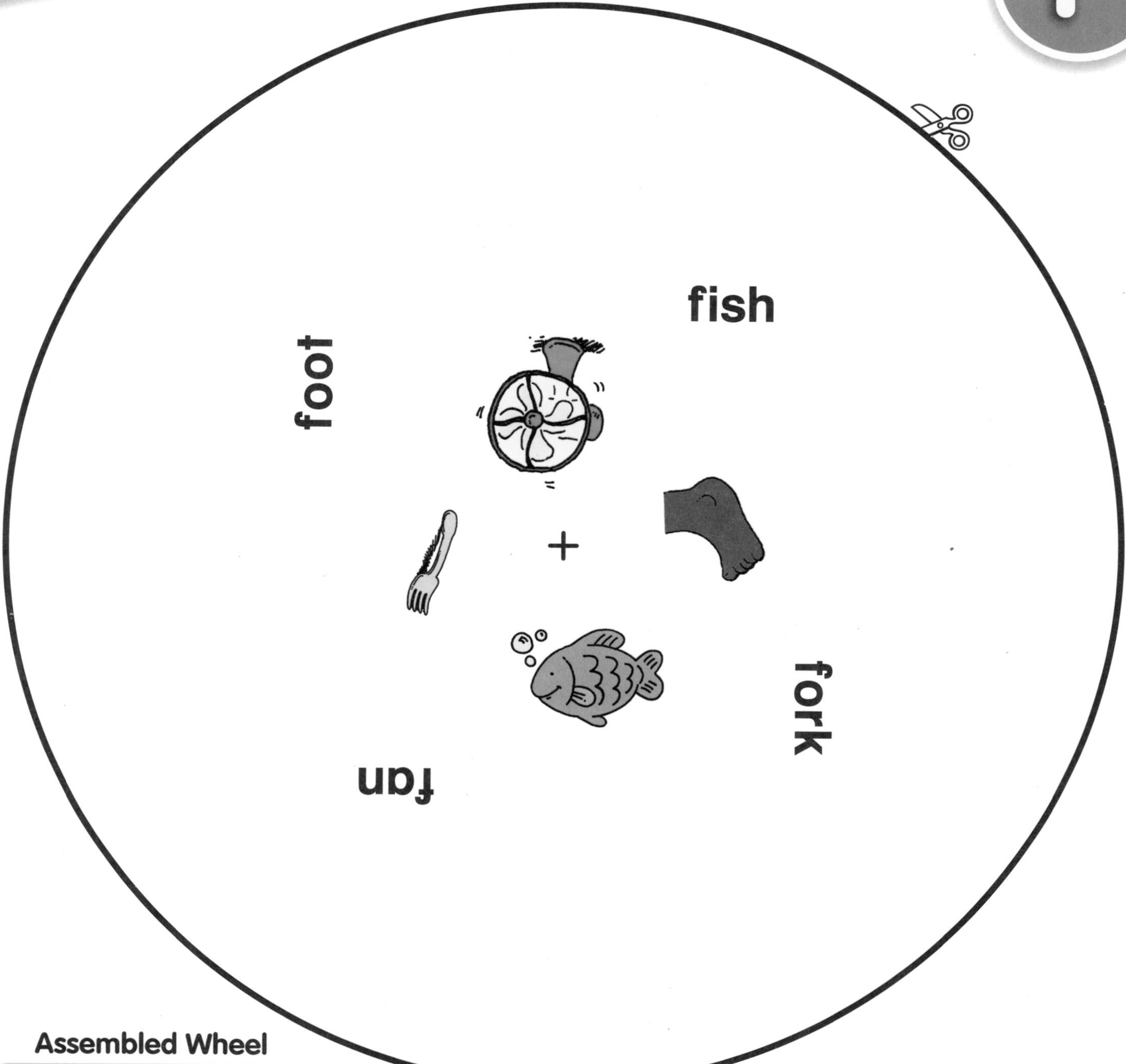

fish

foot

+

fork

fan

Assembled Wheel

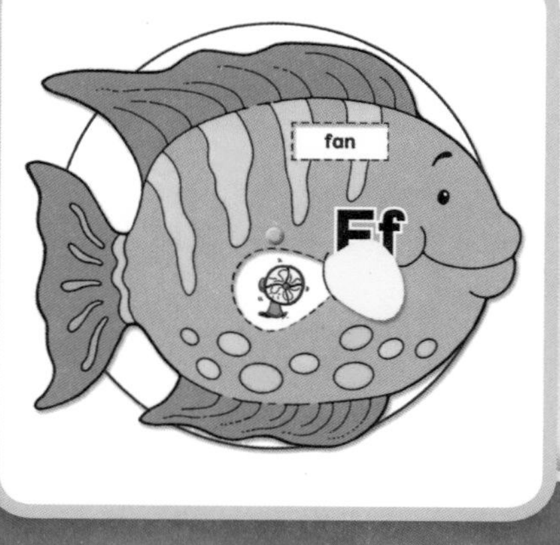

fan

Ff

Gg

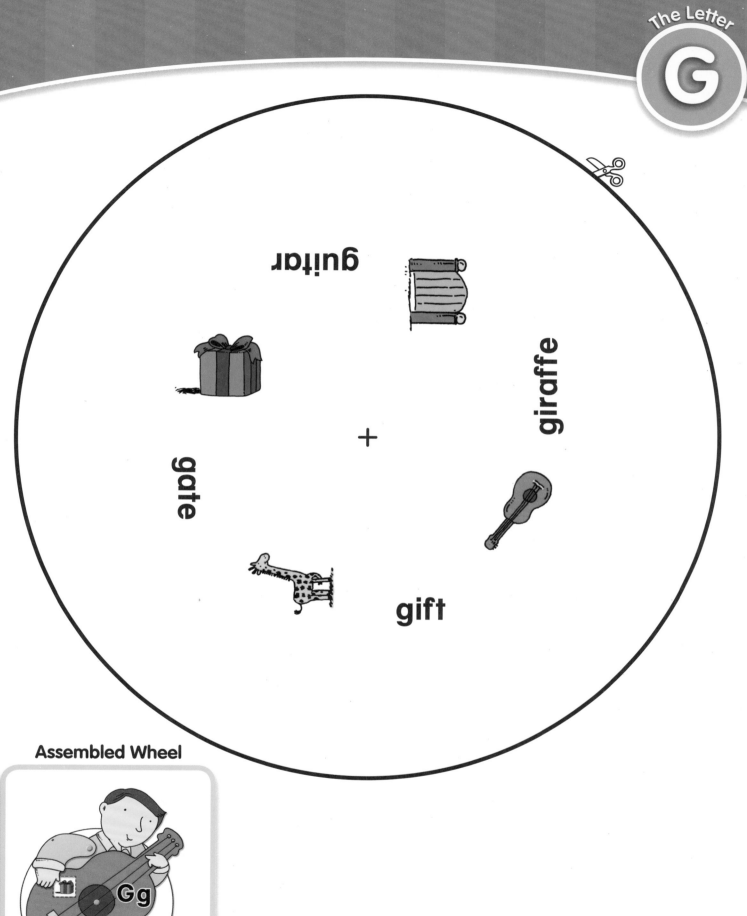

guitar

giraffe

gate

+

gift

Assembled Wheel

Gg

gift

Hh

ʇɒɥ

hamster

+

heart

helicopter

Assembled Wheel

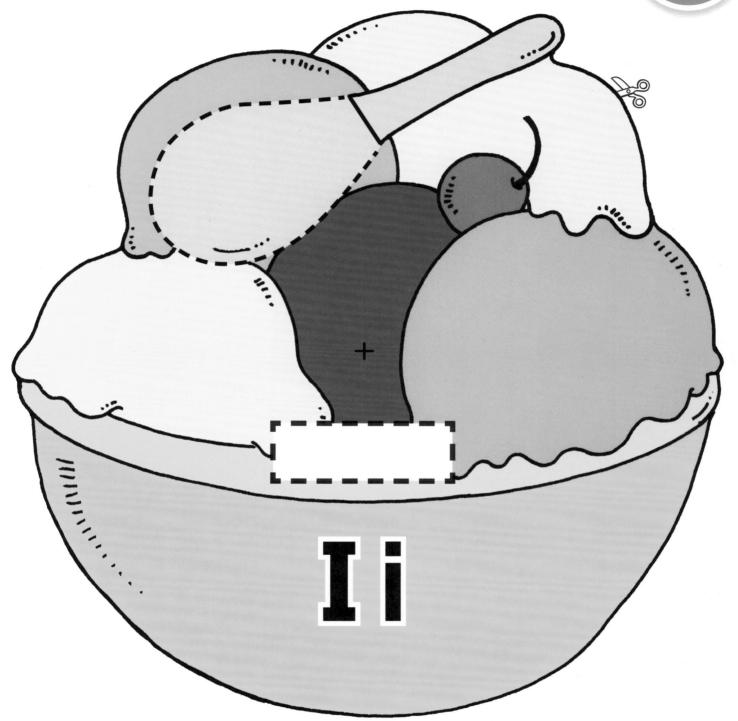

I i

Turn-to-Learn Wheels in Color! Alphabet © 2009 by Virginia Dooley. Scholastic Teaching Resources

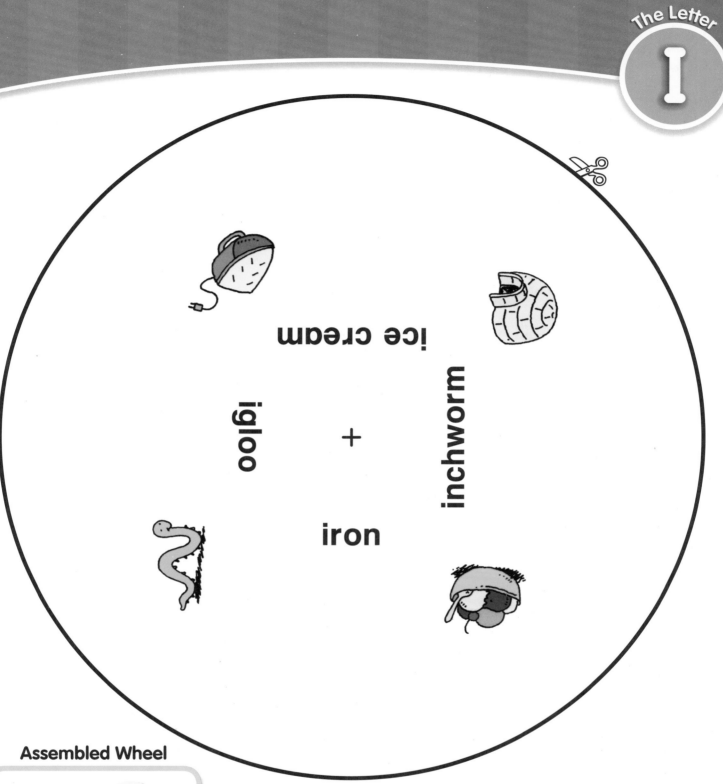

ice cream

igloo

+

inchworm

iron

Assembled Wheel

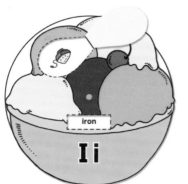

iron

I i

JJ

jump rope

jack-o-lantern

jet

+

jacket

Assembled Wheel

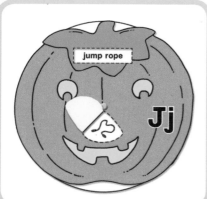

Kk

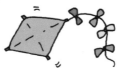

king

kangaroo

+

kite

kitten

Assembled Wheel

kitten

Kk

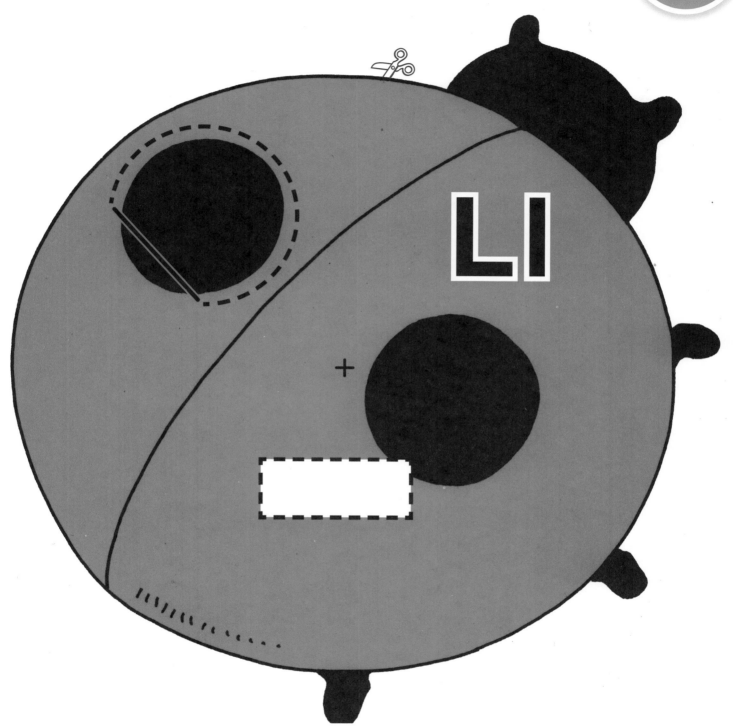

Ll

+

ladder

ladybug

+

lamb

lion

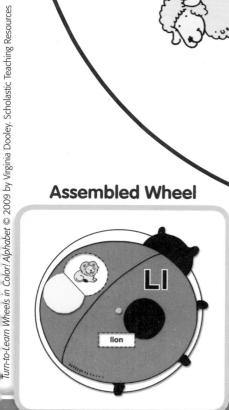

Assembled Wheel

Ll

lion

Turn-to-Learn Wheels in Color! Alphabet © 2009 by Virginia Dooley, Scholastic Teaching Resources

mitten

mailbox

+

mouse

muffin

Assembled Wheel

Nn

nest

nail

+

net

nose

Assembled Wheel

nose

Nn

Turn & Learn Wheels in Color: Alphabet © 2003 by Virginia Dooley. Scholastic Teaching Resources

Oo

uɐǝɔo

octopus

+

ostrich

overalls

Assembled Wheel

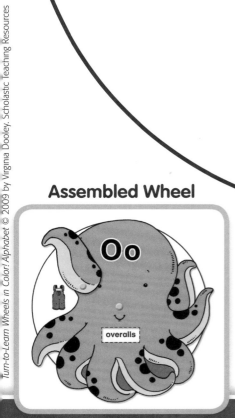

Pp +

✂

uınbuǝd

penguin

pencil

+

pie

pail

Assembled Wheel

Qq

quilt

quart + quarter

ʋәәnb

Assembled Wheel

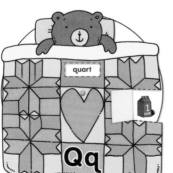

Turn-to-Learn Wheels in Color! Alphabet © 2009 by Virginia Dooley. Scholastic Teaching Resources

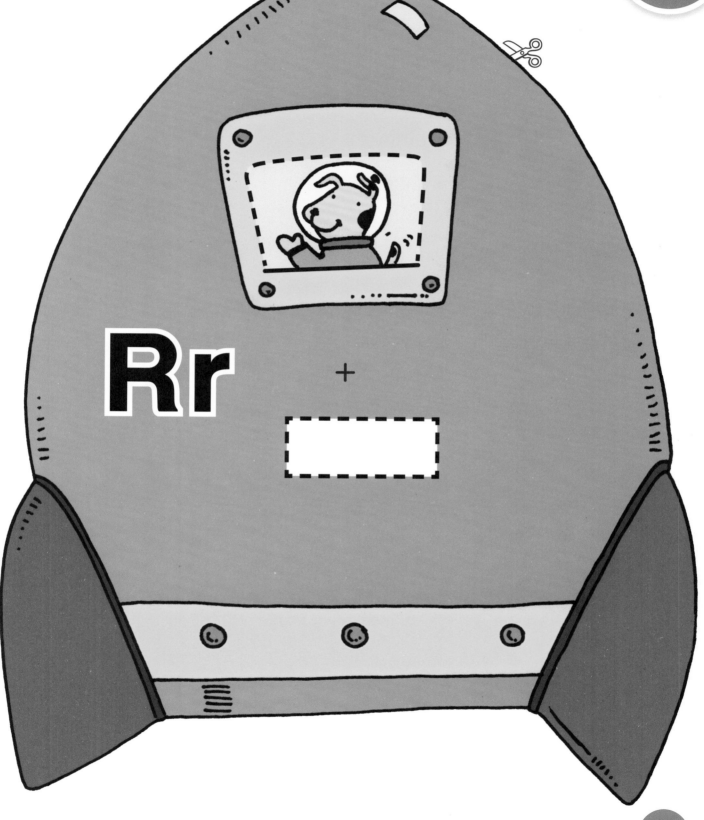

Rr +

x

rocket

rabbit + ring

rug

Assembled Wheel

Rr

rug

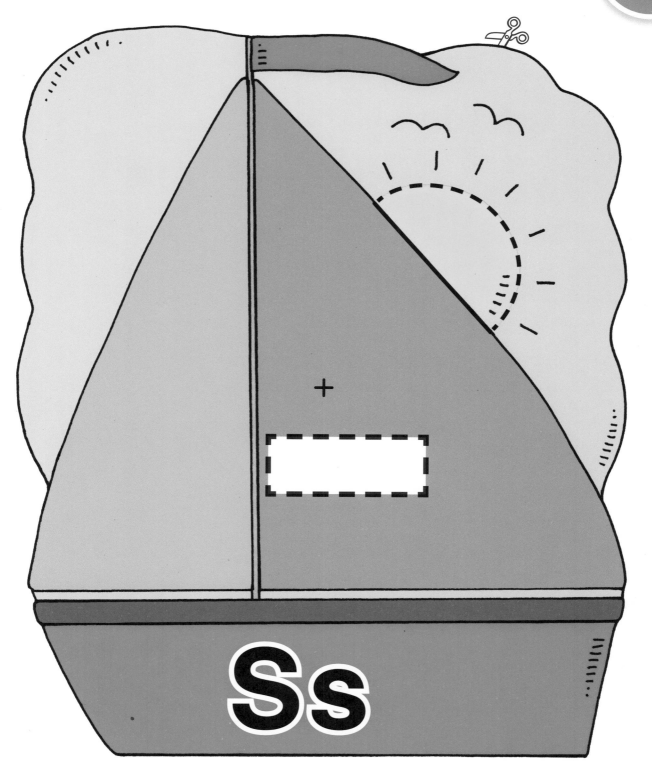

Ss

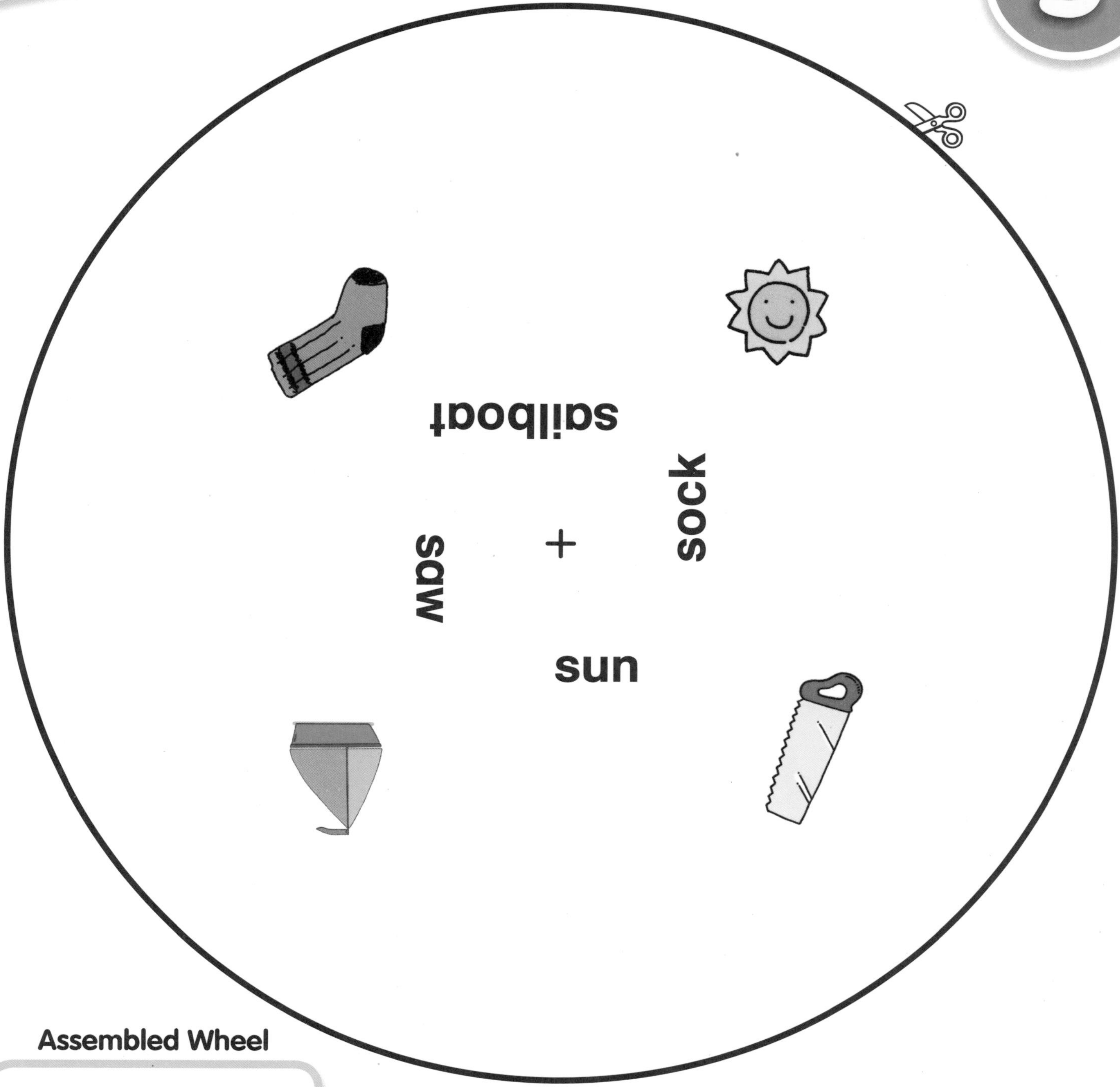

✂

sailboat

sock

saw

+

sun

Assembled Wheel

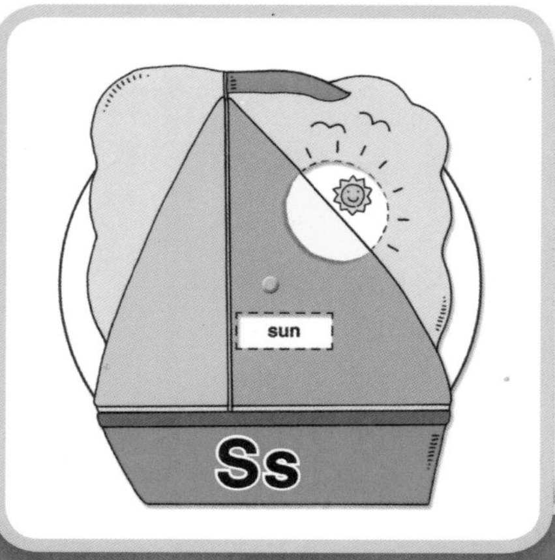

sun

Ss

Tt   +

tiger

turtle

+

table

tent

Assembled Wheel

Uu

umbrella

upstairs

+

unicorn

unicycle

Assembled Wheel

Uu

unicycle

van

valentine

+

vest

violin

Assembled Wheel

Ww

wheel

wagon

+

whale

watch

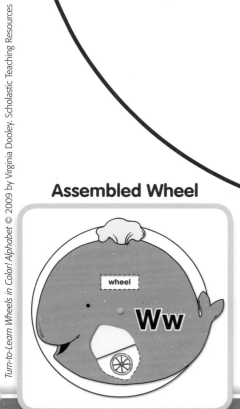

Assembled Wheel

wheel

Ww

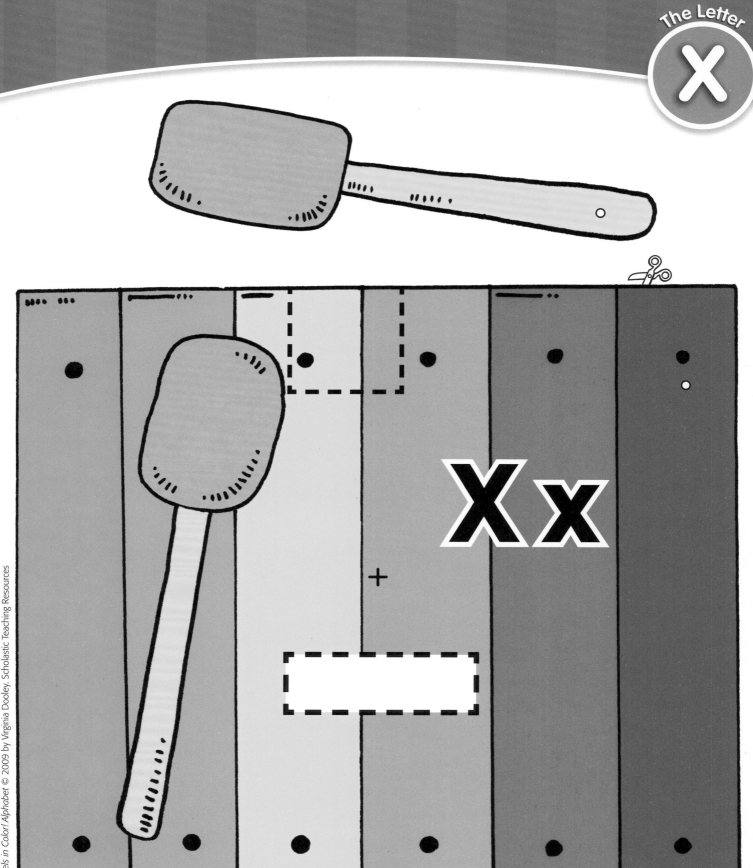

Xx

+

xylophone

box

+

fox

x-ray

Assembled Wheel

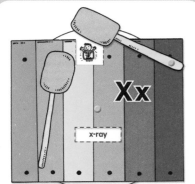

Xx

x-ray

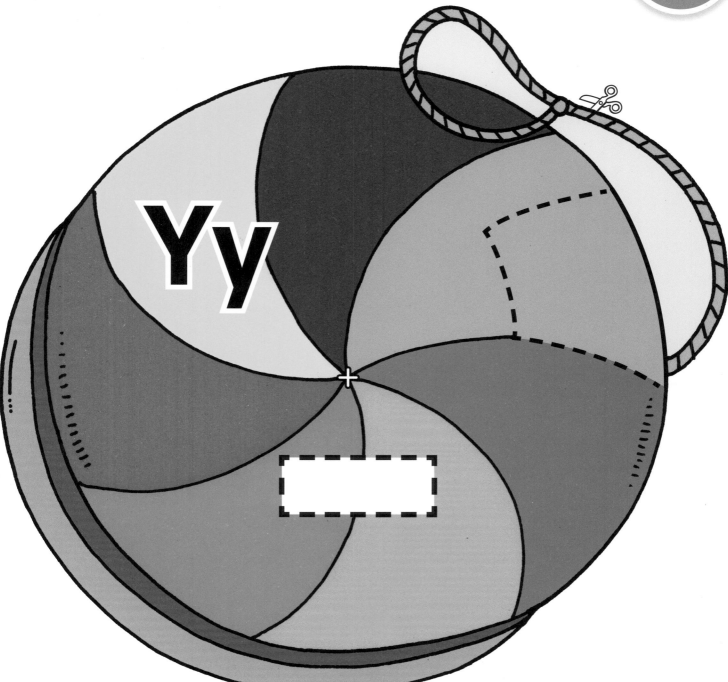

Yy

yo-yo

yogurt

+

yarn

yolk

Assembled Wheel

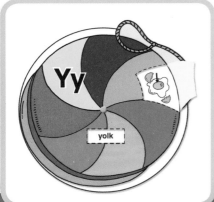

Zz

zipper

zoo

+

zebra

zigzag

Assembled Wheel

Turn & Learn Wheels in Color: Alphabet © 2003 by Virginia Dooley. Scholastic Teaching Resources